Understanding Fear, Anger and Worry

Understanding Fear, Anger and Worry

Michael White's "Absent But Implicit"

BY JODI AMAN, LCSW-R

jodiaman.com

Facebook.com/jodiamanlove

Instagram @jodiamanlove

YouTube Jodi Aman

Twitter @JodiAman

Pinterest JodiAman

Published by: Ja'Love Books
919 S Winton Rd.
Rochester NY 14618
This book is available at quantity discounts for educational use. For
further information, please contact author at info@jodiaman.com.

Understanding Fear, Anger and Worry is designed to provide
practical recommendations to ease anxiety suffering. It is not meant
to replace the medical or mental health advice of your current
provider. If further assistance is required, the services of a local
competent professional should be sought.

10 9 8 7 6 5 4 3

Aman, Jodi. Understanding Fear, Anger and Worry: Michael White
Absent But Implicit –Second Edition. pages cm

Include bibliographical references.
ISBN: 978-0-9985613-2-5 (paperback)
ISBN: 978-0-9985613-3-2 (ebook)
1. Anxiety 2. Self Help 3. Mental Health 4. Psychology

Many names and identifying characteristics of people mentioned in
this work have been changed to protect their identities.

Contents

Jodi Aman

Introduction: Noticing what is precious in our laments:

In the context of everyday conversations, it is all too common to hear expressions of complaint, pain, frustration, worry, and/or anger. In our culture, we are quick to point out what we don't want and what we don't like. These expressions, and the thoughts that go with them, plague our lives, infiltrating our minds and our bodies, making us feel lonely, helpless, scorned, despairing, and even physically sick.

These expressions have the potential to depress the speaker as well as bring down everyone listening. When expressed, the belief becomes its own little truth:

> This isn't fair!
>
> Why does he have to treat me this way?
>
> I can't catch a break.
>
> Nobody understands.

When thought and expressed, it becomes the way it is: "I am guilty." This truth status limits any movement outside the proclamation, thus exacerbating the predicament. It is definitive: *I am miserable*. And that is that. Period.

How would we hear those complaints differently if we knew that in the shadows of them, there was something that person held precious? "I am miserable," is a thin statement, but can tell multiple stories for those who double listen. Michael White (White, 2000) invites us to double listen, hearing both the expression and what's absent from the expression but implicit in its meaning. The preciousness is not publicly stated in "I am miserable," but that doesn't mean it is not there.

What is implicit about complaining that you are miserable? That you wish you weren't. It is a desire for another way of being; for example, being happy. The desire for happiness is being held precious. This already invites a new view of complaints. But White takes it even further. He asserts that if we desire to be happy, we must know something about being happy.

There must be some knowledge or familiarity with it for us to know we want it—sometime in the past that we either felt it or observed it in someone else, or we wouldn't know that we wanted it.

To know misery is to know its opposite, happiness. One cannot exist without the other. Without knowing happiness, misery would feel, well, neutral. We only understand misery as it is different from happiness and happiness as it is different from misery. Understanding this can make all the difference in how to position ourselves in our complaints. Read the following example:

Pain as a testimony - Amy's story

In my work as a therapist, I met with a fifty-seven-year-old woman, Amy, who was abused by her brother when she was seven years old. She began a session with the following questions and requests: "Why did sexual abuse have to screw up so much of my life? Why does it have such a long devastating effect on a person's life? I want to know. I want you to tell me!"

Curious about the context of her "screwed up life" and the "devastating effects" she was referring to, I asked about this. She told me of an intense pain that followed her everywhere in every part of her life. There were times she felt this pain so pervasively that it kept her, either up all night or in bed for days. Not only had it brought her to tears for hours, but it also complicated and exaggerated physical ailments, including back, shoulder, and leg pain. "Above all," she said, "I am afraid I will suffer forever."

Even though her descriptions were detailed, I knew there was something absent in her expressions of pain, but implicit in their meaning. Her pain is in relation to something. It is a longing for some treasure and/or a hope for something important to her. The pain of abuse is related to what it was the person treasured that was violated by the abuse. In addition, the intensity of Amy's pain is a testimony to how precious she held said treasure. I posed a question to see what this might be.

> **Me:** Can I ask you, when your brother did this, what was it that the abuse stole from you?
>
> **Amy:** He took my innocence. He took my joy. He took my joy of life, and then it was gone… I had no joy! None!

Amy quite quickly named what is "absent but implicit" in the pain she was experiencing, but I decided to clarify it again to highlight it. The "screwed up life" and the "devastating effects" had had loads of airtime. It was crucial to make more meaning around the joy to give it some story and power.

> **Me:** Would you say that joy is precious to you?
>
> **Amy:** Yes!

To highlight it even more, I asked her to quantify this preciousness.

> **Me:** How precious?
>
> **Amy:** Very, very important to me.

To ensure a multistoried conversation, I acknowledged the pain and began the process of giving this pain new meaning.

> **Me:** Is the longevity of the devastation related to how 'very, very' precious joy of life is to you?
>
> **Amy:** Yes! Yes!

Curiously, I wondered if she had made it through fifty years without joy at all. Absolute joylessness was improbable, so I questioned her to find traces into some stories of joy that ran counter to the problem story ("screwed up life"). If there was joy at all, I was eager to learn how and why she allowed it to return to her life.

> **Me:** Has there been a time, when joy started to come back in your life, even a little?

In response, Amy shared a story of when she was a pregnant teenager, away from home and in an abusive relationship. Out of her apartment window, there was a bird's nest with a mother bird warming her eggs. Over a period of weeks, she watched the bird often and felt as though the bird was watching her, too. It was almost as if they were cheering each other on as they prepared for motherhood. Amy said watching and connecting to this bird gave her incredible joy. "Perhaps," she said, "the first joy I felt since I was abused."

She told many more stories about her connection to nature and animals from trees to woodland creatures. For example, to beat off her midwinter depression, she would walk in the woods and follow animal tracks. She did this playfully and joyfully.

As she was relaying these stories, more and more joyful times came into her memory, mostly involving children, animals, and the earth. We wove these tales together around the theme of joy into a rich story of her holding onto this treasure despite the abuse. In these conversations, we re-authored the story of her life from "screwed up" to "empowered to find joy." These stories also led us to new identity conclusions, from being —scared, and —messed up to being a "steward of the earth," an "advocate," "compassionate," "committed to kindness," and "committed to children."

Amy was initially surprised, yet heartened, that she hadn't let her brother take all of her joy, that she held onto it through all these years. Through many hard times in her life, when joy felt scarce to her, she knew exactly how to find it in nature and in children.

This was a much more empowered position to reflect upon her life. Remembering these stories and giving them meaning offered her greater access to the skills she has in finding the joy she desperately desired. Her initial explicit expression, "Why does sexual abuse have to screw up so much of my life? Why does it have such a long devastating effect on a person's life? I want to know. I want you to tell me!" implicitly expressed her desire for joy.

Previously her brother and this lament held all the power. Thinking that we have no joy, definitively, prevents us from seeing or feeling it. This conversation took the wind out of the sails of that lament. Now, knowing she had access to joy, she felt empowered.

To her, this meant she did not fully give in to the fear that she "will suffer forever." She held onto hope as she engaged in these joyful scenarios, hope that she could feel better. For the most part she has learned not to give into the fear in the present either. She continues to seek out, practice, and work on ways to help herself feel better every day. Giving her more access to her skills in finding joy, and a way around the "truth status" that her life is "screwed up," this conversation will help her next time she has a hard day.

Now that joy was explicit, I became interested in "peopling" her journey. When we think of one thing definitively (i.e., "It's hopeless."), isolation emphasizes and gives evidence for the "truth" of the despair. We stay in our minds where the problem story runs rabid, building and growing until we feel crazy. Inviting others or the voices of others into the story invites new meanings about ourselves and our situations. These new meanings are powerful in untying the devastating "truth" the dominant problem binds us to. We can see other possibilities.

I began "peopling" her journey with folks from her past. Amy's stories were peppered with children and animals (*animaling* her journey), and I wanted to bring forth their voices to counter her isolation. Following White's **Re-Membering Conversations Map** (White 1995; Hedtke and Windslade 2004), I asked Amy to speak about how each of these contributed to her life and how this contribution might define her. Then I asked Amy to tell me what would the children and animals tell me about her contribution to their lives. Amy tentatively spoke about how their lives might have been impacted by these interactions. This was the first time she thought of how she contributed to their lives, how their lives were altered and enriched by having known her. They became acknowledging witnesses and participants of her reclamation of joy. This acknowledgment creates more meaning, "thickening" this new story of joy. Thickening means developing the story as in making it more robust and sustaining.

Next, I found witnesses to her stories in the present by inviting other people to listen to me interview Amy. I might have used a colleague or a member of her family, but in this case, two other women who had also been abused in their families joined us one afternoon. Amy publicly and explicitly told her stories of joy again, and then I interviewed these women about what they heard. Their reflection provided rich acknowledgment and exponential sustenance for her skills in finding joy. This follows White's **Definitional Ceremony Map** (White, 2000).

This is only a portion of Amy's therapeutic conversations. In months to come, we continued to make new meaning around the abuse, Amy's responses, and subsequent pain and recovery. The above conversations, getting at what is "absent but implicit," were pivotal in her healing journey. We referred to it often.

Amy has since left therapy. She recently came back as a witness and support to another young person I was working with who was abused by her brother. At the end of this conversation, Amy sat proud of her accomplishments and said, "I really have a good life now."

Theory of "Absent but Implicit"

White found inspiration for his application of the "absent but implicit" into therapeutic conversations through Bateson, Derrida, and Foucault (Bateson 1980, Derrida 1978, Foucault 1980). These relational theorists understand that the definition of something derives from its relationship to others things. So the name of something is recalled in memory, not only as the thing named, but also as how it relates to what is around it. (Bateson, 1980, Derrida, 1978).

A pen is not recalled in memory as just a pen. There is an interaction in parts of the mind and recognition is triggered by how the pen is different from other things. Derrida uses the word *differance* with an "a" (Derrida 1978). He says everything relates to its spatial and temporal meaning by relation to what it is not. The *differance* is the distance between what something is and what that thing is not. For example, the table is only a "table," because it is not the space around the table or because it is not a "chair." The differance is the distance between the "table" and the "space," or the "table" and the "chair." One can only make meaning of "table" as it is not space, chair, or anything else for that matter. This is opposed to ideas of essentialism, which states that truth has an essence with self-sufficient elements (Gelman, 2005). Essentialists believe the table can be defined by its own elements, instead of how it relates to the rest of the world.

Relational theory also poses that perceptions and understandings of the table could be different depending on who is noticing it due to that person's experiences with tables and how tables relate to that person's history. For example: did they eat with a joyful family around a dinner table each night? Was the table piled with junk and everyone fended for themselves for dinner? Did they grow up in a culture that sat on the floor? How can a table ever just be essentially a table, when there are so many relational meanings that can influence our perception of "table?"

White applied this understanding to therapeutic conversations. People often come to therapy with an account of their life that is problematic. This problem story is often dominant in that it takes up much space and energy in their lives: affecting their mood, the view of themselves, and their understanding of the world.

When people are experiencing problems in life, those problems are also related to something. It is often because of this relationship that they are problems in the first place. It is a problem in so much that it is not whatever else they want. For example, losing a loved one is a loss in relation to the previous presence of that loved one. Rejection is a problem because it is not the desired acceptance.

White assumed the co-existence of other stories, subordinate to the dominant stories, but very much present (i.e., wanting a loved one, wanting acceptance). He built his therapeutic approach (Narrative Therapy) on bringing these subordinate stories forward and richly developing them to give them power and energy. Developing these stories manifests shifts in people's worldview. In creating these stories, they create a new reality they can then step into. In the example above, Amy developed stories of caring for children and caring for the earth.

These stories were already present but did not have much attention in her life. By bringing them forth and adding a wind in their sails, they became more the focus than her joylessness-- not only aiding but steering her journey. She shifted her attention and stepped into this new reality and this improved her mood, her physical experiences, her opinion of herself, her sleep hygiene, and her ability to get along with her family. She now had a solid foundation- her own compassion- rather than the previous story of victimhood--on which to stand on and face the world.

When a problem story seems all encompassing, it may be hard to wade through as if searching for the light from the middle of the tunnel. People sometimes feel overwhelmed by their pain, anxiety, frustrations, and complaints. The darkness of the predicament blocks all possible views of the subordinate stories. White has given us many concepts and "maps of enquiry" to help light our way.

The idea of "absent but implicit" is among his most brilliant guiding torches. He proposes that to fully understand someone's expression, we have to listen to both the explicit expression and what that explicit expression suggests about what is not expressed. What has been left out of the explicit expression is what is referred to as the "absent but implicit." (The desire for connection in "loss," the desire for success in "failure," the desire for safety in "fear.")

The absent but implicit meaning in an expression is the understandings, experiences, and histories that help a person make meaning of the original expression. For example, a person cannot express despair without some knowledge, understanding, or history of some kind of hope because despair can only be understood in its relation to hope. When "hope" is named, we know there is some history or familiarity with it. Asking about this history and knowledge of hope shines the light onto a pathway to new ways of thinking and understanding. Enlightening the history enlightens the future. It is an access into a *preferred* storyline and can lead one out of the tunnel.

In the shadows of every complaint, the absent but implicit tells of what is precious to the person that has been lost or threatened. The intensity of the complaint is a testimony to how precious it is. When we are complaining, the complaint receives the focus of our attention. We may think that we want validation for our feelings, but this only justifies the negative. We are better off with validation for what we value (which may be totally hidden before this point.)

This feels so much better since it has been undervalued which is why we are upset. These absent but implicit conversations intend to bring into focus and acknowledge what is precious.

A client of mine told me of a strong urge he recently felt to "keep driving" when he was emotionally overwhelmed. He assumed this was pathological and meant that he was "going off the deep end." However, he told me (once I asked) how this was "an act of wanting to separate himself from the terrible feelings he was having." I wondered: *Wouldn't anyone want to do this if the feelings are so bad?* Looking at it this way, his desire was a step in the right direction rather than regression. He could now tell me that he'd be crazy if he wanted to stay with these feelings, they were so horrible. If I validated his feelings that he was pathological, I might have missed his desire to feel better and build on this.

Jodi Aman

History

White first presented this idea at the Narrative Therapy and Community Work Conference in 1999, which was later written up in an article called "Re-Engaging with History: The Absent but Implicit" (White 2000). He was particularly interested in these ideas in his last few years and, even more vigorously, his last few months of life. In workshops, just before his death in 2008, he was promising his students a more formalized 'map.' Regretfully, this was not completed.

However, the informal map that students documented (in note taking) from his lectures survives as our guide. The running joke was that in each lecture, the number of "lines of enquiry" would change, from 7 to 11 back to 8. So, no one "White Absent But Implicit Map" exists.

In 2009, *Family Process* published "The Absent but Implicit: A Map to Support Therapeutic Enquiry" by some of White's senior students, Maggie Carey, Sarah Walther, and Shona Russell (Carey et al, 2009). The authors present a comprehensive therapeutic approach, making a significant contribution to the extension of these ideas.

Like Carey, Walther, and Russell, I too reviewed my notes, compared them to other students, contemplated White's recorded consultations, and reflected on my many years of asking people these questions. The following line of inquiry or "map" came out of this exploration. I presented it at the Narrative Therapy and Community Work International Conference in Adelaide in 2008 and again at the Summer School in Toronto in July 2010.

14

Absent but Implicit Map

Expression is expressed

1. Explore context

2. Explore effects

3. What is the expression in relation to? (Absent but implicit question)

4. Name the "value" - what is precious

   4a. Qualify "value"

5. Ask about history of this familiarity/ knowledge/value

   5a. Link to more stories and intentional state understandings

6. Acknowledge the value by peopling the journey in history

7. Acknowledge the value by peopling the journey in the present and future. That which was absent but implicit becomes publicly explicit.

This map is not a linear step-by-step guide to therapeutic inquiry; it is just a practice tool to help hone skills in expanding curiosity as we develop our own understanding of the absent but implicit. These inquiries can be taken up in any order, combined, skipped, lingered on, intertwined, and/or repeated. Conversations are organic and a therapist's next question relates to the person's response to a previous question. The map is a guideline, a learning tool to expand curiosity, creating new possibilities in our conversations.

Steps 1 and 2: Explore the Context and Effects of Expression

People often see themselves as their problems. For example, "I am a loser." The problem defines them, or is inherent to them, like an illness. There is not much place to move outside this description.

Immobilized and saturated, this way of understanding, called "internal state understandings," (Bruner, 1986) causes people to judge themselves harshly, exacerbating the problem. An internal state understanding is an internalized self-definition. As a definition it can be hard to get rid of.

Inviting people to describe the context of their lives and of their problems counters this judgment. Located in a context, the problem is no longer internalized. There is a reason for it. It came from somewhere, instead of from inside them, so there is less self-blame. In addition, when people can describe their story from an audience position, they see the bigger picture view. This is a new perspective, which can inspire them to respond in a new way.

Understanding the context can also help us understand the effects of the problem; how it has been for this person and what it has meant for him or her. Some problems can negatively impact our lives in many ways. Making these visible and clearly naming the effects take away some power they hold over us.

Even though we explore the absent but implicit to develop rich stories about what is precious, it is important to have multiple storied conversations. Just as it is limiting to solely talk about problems and the problem story, it is equally limiting to talk only about the preferred story. Exploring the context and effects is the visible side of the double description. Without asking and gaining an understanding of this, a person might not feel heard at all.

In addition, these first two lines of inquiry give us hints into what to ask next. For example, if someone describes one of his or her problem's effects as "messing up my relationship," we might be curious about the importance of that relationship.

Step 3: What Is the Expression In Relation To?

This is *the* absent but implicit question and how the expression is turned upside down. People are invited to unpack complaint–see what is behind it, underneath it, within it. This question can take many forms related to the actual explicit expression. Here are some examples:

Keith: I am so frustrated.

Me: What are you frustrated in relation to? What about it frustrates you?

Sue: I give up!

Me: Up to this point, what have you been holding onto that you now feel like you are giving up on?

Mary: You don't understand!

Me: Are you interested in understanding? What do you know about understanding that makes you know it might be helpful to you now?

Beth: I failed!

Me: What did you fail in relation to? What were the expectations you had that you failed to achieve?

With some expressions, the process of unpacking involves a few more steps. Take the following example of conversations with Rick, who was going through a divorce:

Rick: I came here because I am angry. I am so angry! I don't know what to do about it. I've tried everything. I tried medicine. I tried praying. I tried talking to a friend. I cannot stop this anger.

Before responding, my curiosity kicked in. Internally, I brainstormed questions to find out what was important to Rick.

What was the situation that made him so angry? What is he angry about? What is he asking for in prayer? What does he want in his life, if not anger? Is it important to him to know what to do? Why does he keep trying? I asked:

> Me: What are you angry about?
>
> Rick: I am so angry about the divorce.

Of course! I could nod in confirmation. Many people are angry about divorce. This made sense. I understood, but was this the end of the story? No.

While listening to Rick's expressions, I could have stopped here, making assumptions, since I know what we might be angry about. We miss the opportunity to take the conversation to a new place, and discover the implicit meaning. There are many different things about which to be angry when it comes to divorce; losing your family, having less access to your kids, thinking you're a failure, feeling rejection, etc. I was interested in which of these he was most angry about. Knowing what bothered him was crucial to knowing what was important to him.

> Me: Tell me more about what makes you angry about being divorced?
>
> Rick: I am mad that she left me and is living with him and my kids are there and I am alone.

We can still unpack this further:

> Me: What bothers you about them all being together and you being alone?
>
> Rick: This whole time, I just asked her to please tell me the truth about everything. And she didn't. She lied to me about everything.

This is a perfect segue into the next step.

Step 4: Name the Value - What Is Precious?

> Me: You wanted her to tell you the truth?
>
> Rick: Yes, I just asked for honesty.
>
> Me: Is honesty important to you?

I may never have made the connection between Rick's anger and his valuing honesty had I not kept asking. I might have just assumed what might be a common answer, like betrayal. This would have had me completely missing the point and would have risked leaving Rick feeling misunderstood or invisible. (People going through divorce may not need any more of these feelings.) He also referred to more things he later named as important: spending time with his kids and family togetherness. We explored these, too.

Rick was angry because he had invalidating experiences with what was precious to him; honesty, family togetherness, his own sense of worth, etc. In this step we clearly name the value.

Expressions of one thing, suggests some knowledge of, some understanding of, or familiarity with what that thing is not (Derrida, 1978). When someone is complaining, we can assume there is something lost, or dismissed, or invalidated. That something has some significance, value, and importance. For example, if someone was complaining that a task was "pointless," they must know something about things "having a point to them" or they could not understand "pointlessness." Or if someone was complaining an event was "unorganized," there must be some interest in having things organized, perhaps, for example, because disorganized events disrespect people's time. Time is important to them.

This step seeks to define or re-introduce that which their expression is not, (i.e., "having a point," "respecting time") and clearly name it. In this way, the person is making a public proclamation about what they give value to. They are making this implicit sentiment explicit.

19

Step 4a: Qualify Value

To acknowledge the close relationship to Step 4, this next step is labeled: 4a. A distinction between Step 4 and Step 4a emphasizes the power in this secondary step. In Step 4, the value is named. In Step 4a, we ask how important the value is. This further validates it. In answering how important the value is, the person is invited to publicly acknowledge it. This enhances the meaning of it and makes it even more visible -in other words, more validated.

The value is validated by this process. The person who is upset begins to calm down. (S)he is looking at the predicament in a new way, instead of just the dread, appreciating what it is that they want, love, and hope for.

I never regret asking this question, as it steers the conversation. Sometimes a person places little importance on the value, and this signals me that I may be going down the wrong track. It makes me curious about the complexities I hadn't thought about or encourages me to slow down and linger on thickening it up more. Other times, they tell me it is the most important thing in their life.

For example, I might ask: *You said, 'Spending time with your kids is important to you.' How important is that? Is it a little important or a lot important?*

The response can be varied and people can reflect on how the priority changes in different contexts. These are some responses I have heard when asking this question:

- *Yes, it is incredibly important. I love my kids. My kids are my world!*
- *I don't want my kids to feel like they have to be with me or take care of me because I am lonely. I want them to be comfortable being with their friends and their mother.*
- *I do like having a break from single parenting when the kids aren't with me.*

When high importance is placed on the value in response to this question, this increases the validating effects. As aforementioned, the degree of a person's frustrated response is a testimony to the value of what is being lost or threatened.

The pole metaphor, introduced to me by Karen Young (Young, 2002), helps me visualize this concept. Imagine a flag-less, flagpole with the sun shining on it so that it casts a shadow.

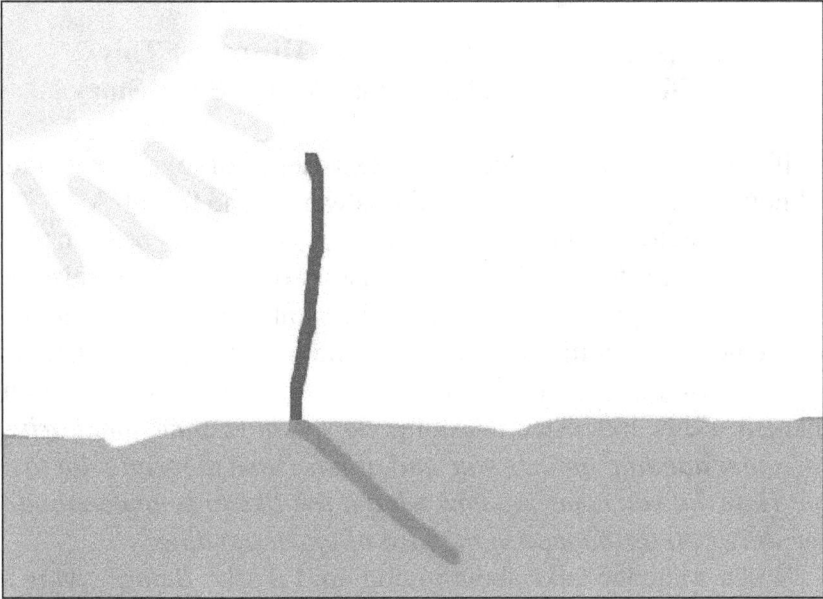

Figure 1

The pole represents the original expression: such as, despair, anger, frustration, worry, pain, etc. The shadow* represents what is absent but implicit in that expression, that which is precious and has been lost, threatened, or otherwise invalidated. There is always something in the shadows of a complaint. In this pole metaphor, the height someone is —up the pole reflects how upset they are. This degree of upset-ness could signify several things: It could signify the preciousness of the value, the circumstances of the loss, and/or the perception of the intensity of the invalidation. When people name the value out loud, it re-validates it. When they qualify the value out loud, it can increase this re-valuing effect, which may lessen the intensity of their upset-ness. "Coming down the pole," so to speak. Absent but implicit conversations bring people down the pole, feeling better and in a terrain that has better views from which to decide what to do next. They can live life from what is important to them instead of living life in their complaint.

Jodi Aman

The shadow is in no way related to the Jungian —shadow. That shadow is something we are less proud of- our darkness. The shadow metaphor I am using means that it is not seen explicitly, but still present. And it represents something valued.

Step 5: Re-Engaging With the History of This Familiarity/Knowledge/Value- Asking For a Story

If we never had knowledge, nor experience of joy, how would we know we wanted it? Where did this want come from? A powerful way to bring the subordinate story of what is precious to the foreground is to enquire into the history of it. There are always stories from our past that will clarify, illustrate, and tell the tale of how we became familiar with the idea and learned to appreciate it in some way. Step 5 asks for this story. For example, if 'understanding' is named, I'd be interested in asking: *So you have some familiarity with understanding, and as you said, it has come to mean a lot to you. How did you come to know what it felt like to be understood? How were you introduced to the idea of understanding?*

When someone talks about giving up, I'd ask: *Before giving up, what was it that you held onto? How was it that you held onto it all this time? Through the hard times in your life, what held this up? How did you hold it close to you?*

From here, the re-authored story begins to develop. Ensuing conversations fill in the details, including the people involved, the way they felt, how they responded, the words in their head that they used to make decisions, what they did before, what they did next, the context, the effects, and more.

While hearing these stories, I listen for "personal agency" (White, 2007) -the sense of being an agent in one's life, rather than a passive recipient of their experiences. Feeling out of control, disconnected to one's agency is often part of a forlorn expression. We often feel a lack of power in being able to affect our situation. Like if someone dies and we did not prevent it and we cannot change it, we might feel separated from our agency.

This map reconnects people with their agency because they can hear stories about how they held onto the preciousness through their life and now feel like they can hold onto the preciousness in the relationship, even though their loved one died. Reconnecting them with their agency empowers them. Hearing stories of how they engaged with what is precious brings their agency into focus.

Sometimes a person relays that they only know joy because they noticed someone else having it. I bring in the agency by asking: *How did you recognize it when you saw it?* Perhaps we became familiar with joy from reading about it in a book, but there must have been some reason we recognized it when we read about it. Our agency is how we related to the joy when we were exposed to it. Did it bounce right off us or did we take it in and let it warm us a little?

Step 5a: Link to More Stories and Intentional State Understandings

Both Step 5 and 5a follow a **Re-authoring Conversations Map**, (White, 2007). Re-authoring conversations link stories around the same theme, clearly name actions, and highlight intentional state understandings (Bruner, 1986, White, 2007). Intentional state understanding, as opposed to internal state understandings, (See **Step 1 and 2: Exploring the contexts and effects of the expression.**) are descriptions about ourselves that describe how we want to be. These are preferred ways to think of ourselves. They go along with the purposes we have for our lives and what is important to us. For example, "Being committed to making people feel special" or "Being compassionate."

Bringing additional stories forth from different parts of a person's history and connecting these to that person's understanding about their own purposes, commitments, values, hopes, and dreams is a powerful agent of change in the present.

Learning the preciousness that stands behind a person's actions, and linking this to their intentions over time, increases experience of re-validating the value. Like Amy, people realize that they have the power they thought was lost to them, since they held on to this preciousness through so much difficulty.

They realize it was never really lost to them, that the abuser or the oppressor in their lives did not take it away, at least not fully. Feeling empowered rather than the victim, shifts power in other areas in their lives, helping them step into more and more stories where joy is present.

Step 6: Acknowledge the Value by "Peopling" the Journey in History

Within these stories from the past, there have been people present the moment the value was introduced to us: a teacher, a beloved aunt, a grandmother, a neighbor. Russian Psychologist Lev Vygotsky proclaims that we do not learn in a vacuum. We learn in relationships, through social collaboration. These people have played significant roles in our journey and our stories of joy, connection, honesty, love, sense of self-worth, or anything else we hold precious. They helped us shape the meaning of these values from the conception of our understanding. Their voices can keep us company, hold us up when we fall, and whisper hope into our ears when we despair. In short, they help us stay connected to them.

"Peopling" a story is bringing forth the energies of these people, their voices, and their thoughts about us (White, 2007). The Re-Membering Conversations map (Hedtke & Winslade, 2004, White, 1997), (See **Pain as Testimony-Amy's Story**) brings forth this acknowledgement. In this line of enquiry, a person uncovers not only how the figure might appreciate their actions in the past but also how they might appreciate the intentional state understandings and actions in the present if they were here.

Bringing forth this energy is exponentially acknowledging in many ways. It appreciates *us*, what we *value*, and our *actions* and steps we took (our agency) in keeping it close to us. Sustaining the worth in all of these sustains our ability to continue to keep it close, in a visible way, where it can ease our minds and our hearts that nobody, but nobody can take it away again! In fact, no one ever did.

When people experience a trauma, they often feel disconnected to who they were before the trauma. They may feel forever and completely changed by what happened. These absent but implicit conversations reconnect people with themselves by connecting them to what was important to them.

If something is important to them now, there is usually some trace of that importance in their history. Feeling reconnected with their pre-trauma selves by what they treasure, profoundly decreases the effects of the trauma (Denborough, 2006). Often the ways people survive the trauma experience are clues into what they value. For example, they distract their abusive parent, even though they will "get it" to protect a younger sibling. Lifting up this value (children deserve protection) can be a crucial piece of trauma recovery.

Peopling a story can also counter isolation. Isolation supports problems and can have a crippling effect on a person's sense of self. How we know ourselves is from what is reflected back to us by people around us. We are a self only in relationship to others.

If we have experienced abuse, the voice of the abuser remains loud. We want to de-populate our mind with this voice, since it will create a small and poor sense of self and an even lower self-esteem. This is easier when our life is then repopulated with preferred voices: for example, a grade school teacher who saw the good in us. In contrast, this gives us a robust sense of self by filling up the empty spaces and helping us see ourselves through the eyes of someone who loved us.

Step 7: Acknowledge the Value and Peopling the Journey in the Present and Future.

Having these voices from the past can be really helpful, but it is also important to make sure our present life is populated with a supportive community, too. Even with this preciousness validated we can easily fall into old habits of despair when in isolation.

Rick and I (See **Step 3: What Is the Expression In Relation To?**) continued talking about honesty once he named it as what was important to him. The conversation brought forth a history of his relationship with integrity, his intentional state understandings, and how he ameliorates the value in his own life as well as taking the higher ground with his ex-wife. He felt calmer and a bit more robust, but his anger still loomed. He was interested in relieving his anger more and became frustrated that his ex didn't validate him.

It is not uncommon to desire validation from the person who hurt us most. However, while it is not impossible, it is unlikely that person will pro-offer it. If we cannot count on the 'ex' for validation, what can we do to let go of our anger? We can get an audience (outsider witnesses) of family, friends, or others with insider knowledge (people who have experienced in their past what we have experienced). Being deeply acknowledged by those who care, appreciate us, and understand is a powerful healing process. This rich acknowledgment of our very selves can dissolve our anger.

I offered Rick a Definitional Ceremony (See **Pain as a Testimony- Amy's Story**) inviting other men whose ex-spouses had cheated on them to listen while I interviewed Rick about his integrity, kindness, good moral choices, and the history of these amidst the context of this huge betrayal. Following this, the men responded by reflecting Rick's story back to him. These men reflected on what caught their attention, what images came to their mind when listening, what experiences they had that made these particular expressions resonate in this way, and finally where they were in their hearts and minds after hearing this conversation between Rick and me (how they are different upon hearing it). This acknowledged him in a way I could never do alone. It not only sustained him and his continued good decisions, but also provided relief of his anger.

In this final step, that which is 'absent but implicit' becomes present and publicly explicit. That which is precious is held tenderly again, rather than being threatened, thrown on the ground and stomped on by the contexts of our lives. As well, other people are holding it with us, so there is less threat should it be discarded again. Like elephants gathering around an injured herd member to protect it, our people and their voices stand around us, telling us we are precious. This is an easier place from which to live life.

An Exercise in Noticing the Unlimited Possibilities

Read the following list of common expressions and imagine what might be absent but implicit in them:

I feel hopeless. I am lonely.

The despair is overwhelming. I'm worried.

I have trust issues. I am angry.

I am disgusted. I feel guilty.

I am ashamed. It is so painful.

I have nothing to look forward to. You don't understand.

You're not listening. I'm sick of it.

I give up.

I won't let go.

I'm embarrassed.

We never have sex anymore.

We do not always know what people are holding precious, but brainstorming the possibilities will spark our curiosity, inspiring us to ask. Now make your own list and continue to notice the "absent but implicit" everywhere.

Absent but Implicit As Conflict Dissolution: Conversations with Katie and Jim

The absent but implicit is helpful in dissolving conflicts. In fact, it is a helpful concept when navigating any relationship. When people are feeling high on the pole of upset-ness (See **Figure 1**), they usually express their frustrations from this position (up the pole). This causes conflict since the other hears the expressions from high on the pole.

For example, a heterosexual couple that I met with told me of their increasing experiences with arguments and conflicts. The woman, Katie, complained that her husband was selfish and he only cared about himself. The man, Jim, complained that Katie was mean to him. Katie heard Jim's complaint. Jim heard Katie's complaint, and it became hard to hear anything else past that point. They were speaking from the pole and consequently only seeing each other, and themselves, through their position at the top of the pole. They ended up not liking each other or themselves. (See **Figure 2**)

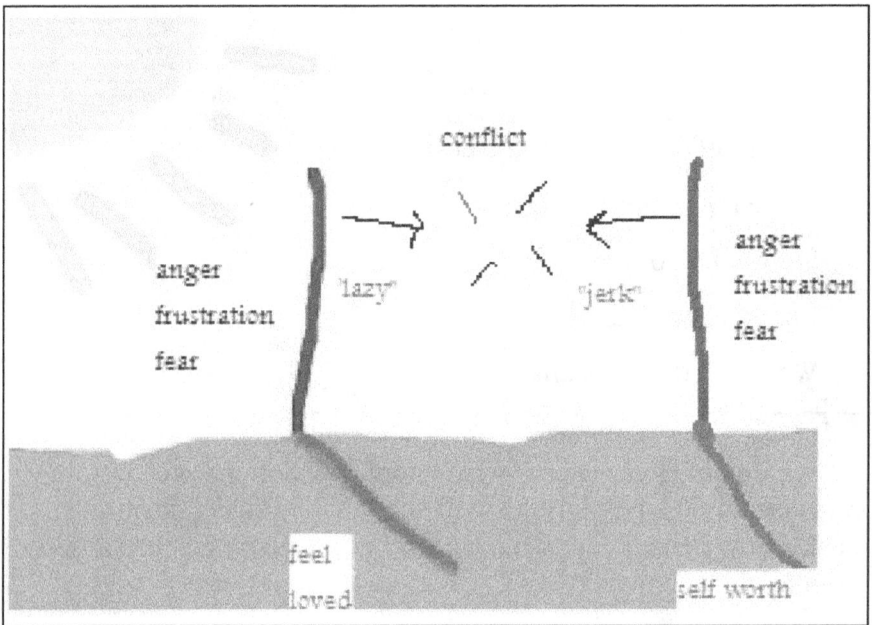

Figure 2

Conflicts can get out of hand quickly. This is a hazard of communication theory. This couple could have expressed these sentiments to each other until they were blue in the face, and instead of resolving anything they would have ended up being more miserable because these expressions lead to negative identity conclusions. In other words, Katie felt identified as "mean" and Jim felt identified as "selfish." A stalemate.

Even though they were hurt and worried that they were what the other called them, they defended themselves. The defensiveness came across as offensiveness, and they both appeared *more* "mean" and "selfish" creating a vicious cycle of negative communication. More communication leads to more negative identity conclusions and even more misery. No movement can be made as this "truth status" takes hold. Sometimes couples come to an un-passable space where they cannot see anything else about each other, other than these descriptions.

The absent but implicit map provides a way to dissolve conflicts like Katie and Jim's. It allows them to get some distance from the hurtful comments and speak about what is important to them. The "values" named are infinitely easier to relate to than criticism. People connect over what is valued in their lives, instead of trying to "win" an argument. Being acknowledged for what is important to them makes them feel valued and appreciated.

In the first meeting, I asked Katie and Jim more about the context of the relationship and the effects of this conflict, asking questions such as: *How long have you been together? Do you have any children? What kinds of things do you fight about? When did the conflict start? How is it affecting each of you? How is it affecting the relationship?* I was listening 1) to understand the contexts and effects so that this couple felt heard, 2) for contexts that might concern me, such as discourses of power and entitlement, and 3) for any thoughts, actions, or feeling that might have been absent but implicit in their frustrations in this relationship.

Following the absent but implicit map with each of them, I discovered what was in the shadows of their expressions while the other partner listened. When Katie spoke first, she said she felt frustrated because she felt like she didn't "matter to anyone." She said her friends didn't check on her, her father rushed her off the phone, and Jim did not want to be with her. She missed people caring about her and making her feel like "she counts for something." I was intrigued because she said that she "missed" it. This means she had felt it in the past. I asked her: *When did you feel cared about? Can you tell me about caring relationships? What was it like to "matter to someone" and "count for something"?*

She told me stories about her late grandmother who treated her like she was "worth the world." She also told me that she learned about "loving ways" when she met John because he did "thoughtful gestures" for her. She knew these "thoughtful gestures" meant John was thinking about her even when they were not together. This made her feel loved. Grandma and John made her feel special and cared about deeply and she could see how she made them feel the same way.

The conversation with Katie continued, and we covered lots of terrain. We uncovered some intentional state understandings including her purposes and hopes for her life, among them, "to connect with people and give them love." I heard many stories of Katie's connection and love, and she mentioned that this was the first time in forever that she felt heard - really heard for her specialness. She felt visible.

Turning to John, I asked his thoughts on "loving ways" and "feeling like one mattered." I wondered if these meant something to him as well. I inquired about them as general life "values" rather than Katie's demands and he related to them fully. He thought these were lovely ways of being in the world and they were what attracted him to Katie in the first place.

Before listening to Katie, John had felt like there was nothing he could do "right." He had thought her criticizing him meant that she did not care about him anymore and this felt really bad. He had felt helpless and gave her space. After hearing Katie speak about what was important to her rather than her complaints about him, he felt heartened. Hearing that she wanted to be connected and loved revived John. He no longer felt helpless, as he realized her complaints were a call for love. This was a new perspective, one that made him feel good instead of bad, and from here, he knew how to respond.

We did the same with John's expressions of frustration and Katie was able to relate to this. This allowed us to negotiate the arrangements of their relationship from a connected position rather than a conflicting position. In addition to people from the past, Katie and John acted as witnesses for each other and acknowledged each other's new explicit proclamations of what they held precious.

This way of dissolving conflict can be applied to romantic relationships, friendships, siblings, coworkers, parent/children, or any situation. In fact, I often draw **Figure 2** when I am sitting with families, finding that the visual is helpful in understanding and taking on this questioning themselves.

I use absent but implicit questions anytime my kids complain, accuse me of something, or are afraid. I hope to teach them how to express from the shadows, making these desires visible. They will get a better response from the people around them.

For example, when they were tiny and I placed a bowl of cereal in front of them, they often started crying and accusing me of not putting in enough milk. I had to teach them that instead of complaining, they should ask for what they want. "May I have more milk please?" It is so simple and easy to give them what they desire when I don't feel the barrage of attack. As their self-awareness grew, they were more and more able to see for themselves what was important and ask for that instead of complaining.

Validation and Entitlement

This book wouldn't be complete without some discussion of validation and entitlement in the context of socio-political implications of anger. A sense of entitlement, employed by a person in a power position is often used to achieve or justify anger. For example, "What I say goes and if it doesn't, I am going to be angry." This is a tactic of power, a threat. We can say what is absent but implicit in that statement is that it is important to "get his/her way." However, it is salient to recognize that these conversations have to be taken further, unpacking "control."

There is much more implicit in wanting control. For one, cultural discourses that tell people of privilege that they "are deserving" of whatever they want. The messages we receive from Western gender role, race and socio-economic discourses in combination with commercialism that, "We should get what we want, when we want it, and deserve it simply because we are us," supports our sense of entitlement.

31

"Control" helps those who are privileged maintain the privileged status. These discourses connect being "in control" with a sense of self-worth. So that, "out of control" feels undeserving and unworthy. Uncomfortable, people feel panicked and desperate to regain control and often express this in anger. In attempt to gain control back, they may employ violence.

Much of violence is based in this fear. Ken Hardy links violence in urban areas to a "diss or be dissed" attitude developed from being severely under-valued in our culture (Hardy, 2005). A gun demands respect when respect is not available otherwise.

The tendency to expect "our way" also comes from a disconnection to our personal agency. If we get stuff just because we are us and don't have to do anything, then, wouldn't we feel powerless when we want something and it is not being handed to us? We feel like passive recipients without much sense that we can engage and affect life. This gives us a feeling of being out of control. On the other hand, if we saw ourselves as agents, we'd feel empowered and would be less likely to impose power over others. We might not change what has happened, but changing how we respond and move through it, significantly changes how we are affected by it, how we feel about ourselves and our relationship to others.

Unfortunately, both fear and desire for control is supported in our culture. Americans feel, as the Constitution says, we have the "right to be happy." People in power positions confuse the right to be happy with "entitlement to be in control." We can recognize statements of entitlement when we interact with someone who identifies with a dominant culture (i.e., gender, majority race, majority sexuality, higher socioeconomic status) or is just attempting to have power over others (i.e., "You better tell me the truth!"). These statements act as justification of power over those who are not deemed entitled.

Supporting this in therapy by validating it reproduces and justifies the abuse of power. Rather than validate this, another conversation unpacking these power and control discourses is necessary, making visible where they come from, who supports them and how they affect others. Shedding the light invites people to shift if they are so inclined.

Children often use this tactic in trying to achieve power in situations where they feel they have no power. I want that toy, and my mom said no. There is something absent but implicit in that anger. It is the toy they desire, but also "having control." Acknowledging the preciousness of the toy is easy, but how do we address the entitlement, the expectation of control?

My work with Cindy can illustrate this. Cindy, 9, hates showers and fights vehemently, sometimes as long as an hour before her mother finally pushes her in. She feels "bossed around" and quite powerless. In response, she tries to increase her power by being obstinate, acting afraid, and criticizing her mother. This quickly turned into a "fear of the shower," distracting her mother's attention from the real problem. In addition, her behaviors decrease her sense of control since she has to take a shower anyway and receives other negative consequences for being uncooperative.

Cindy felt powerless and tried to get power. Her degree of "upsetness" was not to how precious it is for her to be dirty, but a testimony to the desire to feel calm and in control. Little did she know before our conversations that she could have enormous power if she got into the shower quickly. In fact, getting in the shower quickly, she soon found out, shifts the mood, events, and relationships in the whole house for the rest of the evening. This is incredible power. Understanding what is absent but implicit in her opposition without validating her violence, and connecting her to her agency made all the difference.

Conclusion

Writing this book on the absent but implicit allowed me to reflect on my work and the application of these ideas to so many scenarios. The limitless possibilities enthuse and encourage me. Even while listening to the most tragic story, I can see the light and know there is a way forward, no matter what. It is extremely precious to me to know this. Holding on to this, I find endurance and hope. There are so many stories of this endurance and hope and many people in my journey that have been present while these became more and more meaningful for me. I am grateful and feel held up by each and every one of them.

Jodi Aman

Mostly, I am grateful for White's extensive contribution to the mental health field. His excitement and passion for a different, more respectful way of therapeutic conversation continues to be contagious. His ideas have spread to most corners of the globe. Literature on White's work and Narrative Therapy can be found at www.narrativebook.com or www.dulwhichcentre.com/au

References

Bateson, G. (1980) Mind and Nature. A Necessary Unity. New York: Bantam Books. Bruner, J. (1992) Acts of Meaning. Cambridge, Massachusetts: Harvard University Press.

Carey, M., Walther, S. and Russell, S. (2009) The Absent but Implicit: A Map To Support Therapeutic Enquiry. Family Process, Vol. 48.

Denborough, D. (2006) Trauma: Narrative Responses to Traumatic Experience. Adelaide, South Australia: Dulwich Centre Publications.

Denborough, D. (2011) Narrative Practice: Continuing the Conversations. New York: W.W. Norton Derrida, J. (1978). Writing and Difference. Chicago: University of Chicago Press.

Foucault, M. (1980). Power-Knowledge; Selected Interviews and Other Writings. New York: Pantheon.

Gelman, S. (2005) The Essential Child: Origins of Essentialism in Everyday Thought. New York: Oxford University Press.

Hardy, Kenneth (2005) Teens Who Hurt: Clinical Interventions to Break the Cycle of Adolescent Violence. New York: Guilford Publications.

Hedtke, L., & Winslade, J. (2004). Re-Membering Lives: Conversations with the Dying and the Bereaved. Amityville: Bay wood Publishers.

Morgan, A. (2000). What Is Narrative Therapy? An Easy To Read Introduction. Adelaide, South Australia: Dulwich Centre Publications.

Vygotsky, L. (1986). Thought and Language. Cambridge, MA: MIT press.

White, M. (1995). Re-authoring Lives: Interviews & Essays. Adelaide, South Australia: Dulwich Centre Publications.

White, M. (1997). Narratives of Therapist's Lives. Adelaide, South Australia: Dulwich Centre Publications.

White, M. (2000). —Re-engaging With History: The Absent but Implicit. In M. White (Ed.) Reflections on Narrative Practice (pp. 35–58). Adelaide, South Australia: Dulwich Centre Publications.

White, M. (2005). —Children, Trauma and Subordinate Storyline Development. International Journal of Narrative Therapy and Community Work, 3&4, 10–23.

White, M. (2007). Maps of Narrative Practice. New York: W.W. Norton.

White, M., & Epston, D. (1990). Narrative Means to Therapeutic Ends. New York: W.W. Norton. Young, K. (2002) Unpacking the Narrative Suitcase Workshop. Hincks Delcrest Institute.

A

About the Author

Jodi Aman knows people. She is a practicing psychotherapist who has worked with 35 people a week for 20 years in Rochester, NY. She got her Master's in Science in Social Work from Columbia University in 1996 and has studied and taught Narrative Therapy around the world focusing on trauma and anxiety recovery.

Jodi films and edits her own YouTube channel and has five online courses with a focus on getting rid of anxiety and empowering people to have more joy in their lives. She plays herself in *The Secrets of the Keys* self-help movie.

Jodi knows anxiety. In her youth she was immobilized by her own panic and anxiety, yet she clawed her way back to life, and taught herself to master happiness. In this bestselling book *You 1, Anxiety 0,* she shows readers how to win their life back from fear and panic, helping them find peace in their days.

As an inspirational speaker, she helps audiences make sense of their lives. She shows how to shift thinking, change unwanted situations, and finally stop the out-of-control downward spiral by releasing that internal self-critic.

Do you want to go deeper with Jodi?

Find out how to work with with her at jodiaman.com

Click "Work with me" at the top!

Anxiety-Free Me!

Me!

5 week comprehensive online anxiety recovery program!

- Group coaching so it is personalized to YOU.
- Connect with a community that lifts you up and understands.
- Learn what anxiety is and why it is so powerful.
- Get practical tips on how to take it down.
- Change the triggers in your brain.
- Find your life purpose. Find yourself.
- Improve your relationships.
- Live happy and at peace.
- 40+ videos, audios and handouts - for life.

Get it here: https://jodiaman.com/online-anxiety-program $297

Anxiety-Free Kids!

Kids!

Online anxiety recovery for parents and kids!

- Immediate access to over 20 videos, audios and fun handouts for you and your child, for life.

- Find out exactly what to do when you can't stand to see your child suffer anymore!

- Kid-friendly videos featuring my baby girl, Miss Lily Aman!

- Hear directly from the horse's mouth as I interview Anxiety herself!

- Access to a private FB group and get support from people who know what you are going through.

- Have fun and feel freedom from anxiety!

Get it here: https://jodiaman.com/kids-with-anxiety/

$37.99

Driving Anxiety Help

Drive

Drive relaxed and in control!

- Feel in control when you drive.

- Drive your family to places where you'd get to spend quality time and create memories.

- Don't miss another party - no matter which part of town it's in!

- Go to that concert or convention with your friends.

- Get to work without the stress.

- Six downloadable mp3s to listen to while you are driving.

- Build a sturdy self-confidence.

Get it here: http://drivinganxietyhelp.com
$24.99

Flying Free From Fear

Fly

Get rid of flying anxiety
with this meditation series.

- Three mp3s to prepare you for your flight.

- Eight more to use while you are flying.

- Start your recovery as soon as you book your trip.

- Feel in control before you fly.

- Put your family first and your fear last.

- Don't miss or avoid another adventure.

- Have more fun in your life.

- See those ancient ruins!

- Fly to whatever you want.

Get it here: http://fearofflying.tips
$24.99